MODERN ENGINEERING MARVELS

3-D PRINTERS

Valerie Bodden

**Checkerboard
Library**

An Imprint of Abdo Publishing
abdopublishing.com

ABDOPUBLISHING.COM

Published by Abdo Publishing, a division of ABDO, PO Box 398166, Minneapolis, Minnesota 55439. Copyright © 2018 by Abdo Consulting Group, Inc. International copyrights reserved in all countries. No part of this book may be reproduced in any form without written permission from the publisher. Checkerboard Library™ is a trademark and logo of Abdo Publishing.

Printed in the United States of America, North Mankato, Minnesota
062017
092017

 THIS BOOK CONTAINS RECYCLED MATERIALS

Design: Kelly Doudna, Mighty Media, Inc.
Production: Mighty Media, Inc.
Editor: Rebecca Felix
Cover Photograph: Shutterstock
Interior Photographs: Alamy, p. 19; AP Images, pp. 11, 15, 17, 23, 25, 29 (top), 29 (bottom); Emmett Given/NASA, p. 21; iStockphoto, p. 5; Mighty Media, Inc., p. 13; Shutterstock, pp. 1, 9, 13, 16, 26, 28 (top); U.S. National Archives and Records Administration, pp. 7, 28 (bottom)

Publisher's Cataloging-in-Publication Data

Names: Bodden, Valerie, author.
Title: 3-D printers / by Valerie Bodden.
Description: Minneapolis, MN : Abdo Publishing, 2018. | Series: Modern
    engineering marvels.
Identifiers: LCCN 2016962781 | ISBN 9781532110870 (lib. bdg.) |
    ISBN 9781680788723 (ebook)
Subjects: LCSH: Technological innovations--Juvenile literature. | Inventions--
    Juvenile literature.
Classification: DDC 600--dc23
LC record available at http://lccn.loc.gov/2016962781

CONTENTS

It's Saturday afternoon, and you can't wait to do your weekend homework. Your assignment is to make a model of your favorite animal. First, you use your computer to design a shark. Then you hit print. You watch as your 3-D printer creates a shark layer by layer out of plastic.

When the printer stops, you examine the shark. Its fins, tail, and even teeth are molded into a model that looks just like the real animal! This is the power of 3-D printing.

3-D stands for three-dimensional. 3-D objects have height, width, and depth. Traditional computer printing is 2-D, or two-dimensional. 2-D printing creates images with height and width, but no depth. In place of ink and paper, 3-D printers use materials such as plastic or metal. Instead of images on paper, they create objects. This includes tools, car parts, and even toys!

3-D printing is also known as **additive** manufacturing. This is because the printed item is made from scratch. Its layers are built up to create a final object. 3-D printing creates less waste

3-D printers are becoming more and more common in schools. They are used in many subjects, such as chemistry, art, history, and biology!

than traditional manufacturing. It also allows people to create **customized** parts and objects from many kinds of materials. A future in which you print your own toys, clothes, and even food is closer than you think!

Prior to computers, people printed images and documents using printing presses, invented in the 1400s. In the 1800s, typewriters were invented. From there, printing **technology** did not change or improve much for more than 100 years. Then, in the 1940s, the first computers were developed.

Early computers were large and used mainly to complete calculations. Their printers did not print words or pictures. Instead, they punched holes to create patterns in paper cards. A decoder machine interpreted the pattern. It printed out the words or numbers the pattern represented.

As developers worked into the 1950s, printing technology improved. The first high-speed character printers came out in 1954. These could print letters and numbers. Around the same time, the first image printers were developed. But the process for image printing with these devices was slow. It did not allow for high-quality graphics.

Printing punch cards was a very slow process.

An improved method of graphics printing came in 1959 with the development of the first plotters. Plotters worked by moving black pens over paper to draw lines or shapes. Later plotters became the first printers to offer colored ink.

As **technology** improved, computers began to appear in more businesses. Some businesses began using dot matrix printers in the 1950s. The printers contained small pins that struck an inked ribbon. This left small dots on the paper that created characters. These printers were faster than other printers of the time. But they were also loud, and their print quality was generally poor.

In 1969, US engineer Gary Starkweather modified a Xerox copy machine to create a laser printer. It used lasers to draw letters and images on a spinning **drum**. Then, **toner** was applied to the drum. The toner stuck to the spots where the laser had shined. The drum then transferred the toner to the paper.

Laser printers were quieter and faster than dot matrix printers. Their print quality was better, too. But laser printers were more expensive. However, over time their price dropped. More businesses began to use them.

By the 1980s, people began buying computers for their homes. At first, most people used dot matrix printers. But in the

The first laser printers cost $3,600! Today, the price has fallen to as little as $100.

1980s, developers perfected a printer they had been working on for 30 years. It was the inkjet printer. These printers had tiny **nozzles** that shot small drops of ink onto paper. Color inks were added in the mid-1990s. By the late 1990s, inkjet printers were widely used in homes and offices.

For most of history, printers were only able to print in 2-D. That changed in 1981, when Japanese engineer Hideo Kodama published a paper about a rapid **prototyping** machine. Kodama's machine was designed to create 3-D prototypes. It built an object by hardening one thin layer of liquid plastic on top of another.

In 1983, US engineer Charles Hull further developed this system. He created a 3-D printer that used **stereolithography**. First, a computer program designed a 3-D object. It then sliced the object's design into thin layers.

The machine printed the layers one at a time. A platform was lowered just below the surface of a tank of liquid plastic. The printer shined a laser onto the liquid in the pattern of the object's first layer. Wherever the laser hit, the plastic hardened. The platform was lowered and the laser hardened the next layer. This continued until the entire object was printed.

Hull continued improving his invention. He sold the first stereolithography machine in 1988. It was very expensive,

CHARLES HULL

Charles Hull was born in Clifton, Colorado, on May 12, 1939. He earned a bachelor's degree in engineering physics from the University of Colorado in 1961. He then began a career as an industrial engineer. In 1980, he took a job with a company called UVP. It made **ultraviolet** lights for curing plastics.

Hull thought it might be possible to print plastics in layers to create 3-D objects. He began developing this idea. By 1983, Hull had developed a machine that could print a small, 3-D drinking cup. Hull went on to found 3D Systems, a company that produces 3-D printers.

Charles Hull is considered the father of 3-D printing.

costing around $100,000! But many manufacturers found these machines worth the **investment**. With traditional manufacturing methods, **prototypes** could take months to make. Hull's machine could make them in days or even hours!

After Hull's invention hit the manufacturing market, other companies started making their own 3-D printers. In the 1980s and 1990s, some companies used powdered plastic or metals instead of liquid plastic. Others developed a 3-D printing method called fused **filament** fabrication (FFF).

FFF printers use a **nozzle** to melt and eject heated plastic filament onto a base. The printers spread the plastic in thin layer after layer. This method was cheaper than **stereolithography**. But the process was slower and not as accurate.

3-D printing **technology** continued to improve throughout the 1990s. But the machines remained expensive. They were used mainly by manufacturing companies to create **prototypes**.

In the early 2000s, multicolor 3-D printers appeared. They allowed for the printing of many colors on a single object. Smaller models of 3-D printers also emerged. Companies used them to create prototypes, **custom** parts, and more. But home 3-D printers were still in the future.

FFF 3-D PRINTER

Most 3-D printers made for home use rely on fused **filament** fabrication (FFF). These printers use several parts to make 3-D objects.

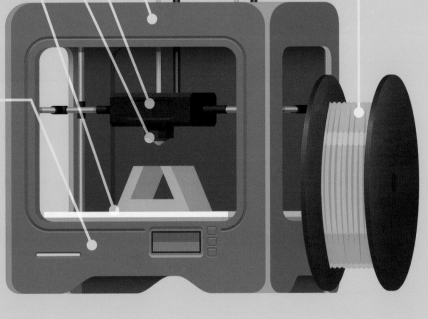

EXTRUDER
This device feeds the filament into a heater block, where it is melted.

HOT END
The melted filament flows through the hot **nozzle** onto the build platform.

BUILD PLATFORM
This is where the printed object is built, layer by layer.

CONTROL BOARD
The control board receives information from the computer and sends it to the printer's motors.

MOTORS
Different printers have motors in different positions. The motors move the build platform or the extruder or both. This controls where the filament is deposited.

FILAMENT
This is the material the 3-D printed part will be made from. It is usually plastic and looks like a thin string.

MAJOR ADVANCEMENTS

3-D printing became more widespread as the machines advanced. In 2005, 3-D printing became more **accessible** thanks to US engineer Adrian Bowyer. Bowyer launched the RepRap project. It designed a 3-D printer that anyone could build.

Bowyer offered instructions for how to build the printer for free online. Anyone could follow the process to design a working 3-D printer. In 2008, RepRap introduced the Darwin 3-D printer. The Darwin was **self-replicating**. Once one was built, it could print the parts needed to build another working printer!

The instructions for creating 3-D printers were now widely available. But not everyone wanted to build their own. In 2008, a company called Shapeways provided another option. People created 3-D designs of jewelry, art, games, and more. Then they sent the designs to Shapeways to be printed and sold.

In 2011, Solidoodle company released 3-D printers for home use. At about $500 each, these printers were more affordable than earlier models. The printers used the FFF method. Users

Josef Prusa has worked on the RepRap project since 2009. He created his own self-replicating 3-D printer, Prusa i3 MK2, that buyers can buy or build themselves.

purchased plastic **filaments** to **insert** in the printer. The printer could print plastic parts up to about 8 inches (20 cm) tall and wide. Other 3-D printer manufacturers soon began developing low-cost home printers as well.

As people began to buy 3-D printers for homes, researchers continued to improve devices made for manufacturing use. In 2015, MIT researchers developed the MultiFab 3-D printer. It used up to 10 different materials to print one object. Among the materials it could print were fabrics, lenses, and **fiber optics**.

The world of home 3-D printing also continued to grow. Some organizations began providing 3-D printing workshops. By the 2010s, many US schools offered 3-D workshops too. Students learned to print objects for projects or experiments.

Museums also use 3-D printing to study dinosaurs. Often, when dinosaur skeletons are found, they are missing bones. But scientists can print the missing bones. Scientists can also print 3-D copies of **fragile** dinosaur bones. This allows them to study the printed bones without damaging the originals.

TECH TIDBIT

In 2013, the Smithsonian Museum in Washington, DC, used a 3-D printer to create a huge statue of Thomas Jefferson.

3-D printers are useful to copy and study historical artifacts, including dinosaur bones and fossils!

PRINTED BODY PARTS!

3-D printers are also used to create parts for living humans. In 2012, a Netherlands patient received a 3-D printed lower jaw. Two years later, a 3-D printed **titanium** hip was **transplanted** into a patient in the United Kingdom. Doctors have also placed 3-D printed **cranial** plates in humans with skull damage.

Medical engineers print 3-D parts for outside the human body as well. 3-D printed hearing aid cases can be **custom**-made for a wearer. Engineers also print 3-D **prostheses** for patients who have lost limbs.

Before 3-D printing, doctors had to rely on products assembled part by part in a factory. Replacement body parts were expensive and took a long time to create. 3-D printing allows parts to be created more easily and quickly. These prostheses are lightweight and relatively inexpensive. They can be easily replaced as a person grows.

Dentists have also used 3-D printed parts in patients. Printers can create crowns and replacement teeth. Some

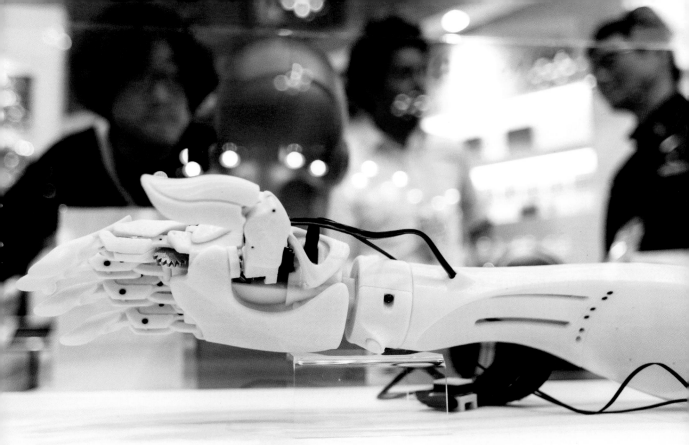

Stratasys displayed its products at the 3D & Virtual Reality Expo in Tokyo, Japan, in 2016. The company offers a variety of custom 3-D printed prosthetics.

orthodontists have even used 3-D printers to make **custom** braces for patients. Many surgical instruments are also 3-D printed.

3-D printing's first use, rapid **prototyping**, remains a major practice today. Many car companies use this method to create prototypes used in testing before mass producing a part. Car manufacturers also print 3-D parts for final products. This allows car designers to create **custom** bodies or engine parts. Some Formula 1 race cars use parts created on a 3-D printer.

Engineers use 3-D printed parts in airplanes too. In 2015, Airbus developed a plane with more than 1,000 printed parts. These parts are lighter and less expensive than traditionally manufactured parts.

3-D printing has even reached space. In 2011, **NASA** launched the Juno spacecraft to orbit Jupiter. The spacecraft includes eight 3-D printed **titanium** brackets used to fasten a rectangular pipe. The pipe sends radio signals to the spacecraft.

In 2014, the first 3-D printer designed for **zero gravity** was sent to the International Space Station (ISS). Astronauts used the printer to create a socket wrench tool and other small items.

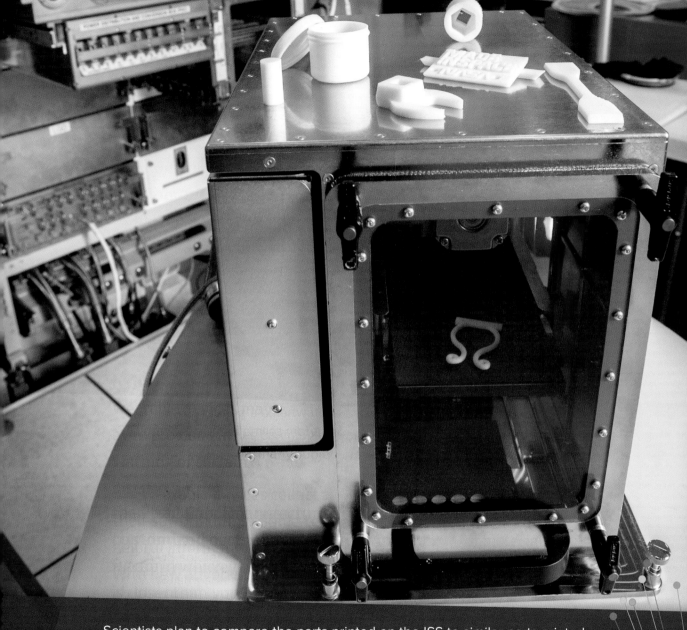

Scientists plan to compare the parts printed on the ISS to similar parts printed on Earth. They want to see if zero gravity in space affects the parts' strength.

Today's 3-D printers can be bigger than a car or as small as a shoebox. Large 3-D printers have created parts for cars, spacecraft, and more. They have printed materials for building homes too. Some are so big that they can print the entire house!

The first 3-D printed homes were built by Chinese company WinSun Decoration Design Engineering. It used a printer that was about 33 by 22 feet (10 by 6.6 m) large. In 2014, WinSun printed 10 small homes in just one day. Panels made from a mixture of glass fiber, cement, and construction waste were printed on site and then fit together.

The company's 3-D printing methods were better for the **environment** than traditional building. Traditional building methods often produce a large amount of industrial waste. 3-D printing **technology** recycles waste products to be used as material for creating more homes, or even bigger projects.

Some engineers envision using 3-D printing to produce temporary homes for survivors of natural disasters. These

homes could be quickly and cheaply printed, and then **demolished** when no longer needed. The material from the demolished homes could then be used to print new ones.

Homes, cars, and even body parts have been created using 3-D **technology**. What might 3-D printers produce next? In the future, you may wear 3-D technology, walk on it, and even eat it!

In 2015, Dutch company MX3D began plans to build a 3-D bridge. It built a robotic 3-D printer able to build structures in the air. The machine can move and will print small amounts of hot steel. The steel will fuse and harden as the robot moves to build the bridge. The project is still in development today.

The same year, researchers developed a new method of 3-D printing called continuous liquid interface production (CLIP). It involves shining an **ultraviolet** light beneath a pool of liquid resin. The light hardens a thin layer of resin as the printer pulls the object upward. This allows more liquid to immediately harden underneath. This method is much faster than standard 3-D printing. CLIP can print some projects in minutes.

Other researchers are working on new materials for 3-D printing. Producing items from recycled material is a major trend

At the age of nine, Jacob Leggette designed several 3-D printed toys. He presented them to President Barack Obama at the White House Science Fair in 2016.

for the future. In-home printing is one aspect of this. Some engineers believe people everywhere may have personal 3-D printers in their homes in the future. They will use the printers to create **custom** clothes, shoes, toys, and more.

More than 278,000 desktop 3-D printers were sold in 2015. The industry earned $5.1 billion in the same year.

New 3-D printing **technology** could also revolutionize future space travel. **NASA** hopes to send astronauts to Mars someday. A Mars mission would take many years. The astronauts would need many supplies. If they had 3-D printers, the astronauts could print the supplies they needed while in space.

3-D printers could even provide food in space. Astronauts could **insert** powdered ingredients into a printer. Then the printer would print out food. Storing powders would take up less space than traditional foods. Powders also keep fresh longer.

Foods printed aboard a spacecraft might sound like fiction, but they may not be far off! The company BeeHex has already printed the first 3-D pizzas on Earth. The printer prints each layer of ingredients separately, including dough, sauce, and cheese. A heated plate bakes the pizzas as they print. The 3-D pizzas can be printed in any shape! Researchers are working on printing other kinds of food, too.

What might the future of 3-D printing look like? Picture using a machine to print a new shirt to wear to school. Next, you set your home's kitchen printer to make you toast and eggs. Remember your plastic shark sculpture? At school, you work with your class to print a life-sized version. With today's advances in **technology**, a similar experience may soon be in your future!

TECH TIMELINE

1959

Plotters print simple shapes and graphics by moving pens over paper.

1980s

After 30 years of development, inkjet printers hit the market.

1940s

The first computers provide printouts in the form of punched cards.

1969

Laser printers are developed. They melt toner onto paper.

1981

Hideo Kodama of Japan designs the first rapid prototyping machine.

2005

The RepRap project develops free instructions for a 3-D printer anyone can build.

1983

Charles Hull builds the first working 3-D printer using stereolithography.

2015

The CLIP method of 3-D printing is developed, allowing for faster printing.

GLOSSARY

accessible–easy to reach, enter, or approach.

additive–something that is added to something else in small amounts.

cranial–relating to the cranium, or skull.

custom–one of a kind, or made to order. Something that is made to order is customized.

demolish–to tear down or destroy.

drum–a cylindrical machine part.

environment–all the surroundings that affect the growth and well-being of a living thing.

fiber optics–the use of flexible, thin fibers to transmit light signals.

filament–a thin, threadlike object.

fragile–easily broken or damaged.

insert–to put in.

investment–the act of putting money toward something in the hopes of earning a profit.

NASA–National Aeronautics and Space Administration. NASA is a US government agency that manages the nation's space program and conducts flight research.

nozzle–a tip on a hose that controls the flow of a liquid.

orthodontist–a type of dentist who specializes in fixing irregularities in teeth.

prosthesis–an artificial device that replaces or adds to a missing body part, such as a leg or arm.

prototype–an early model of a product on which future versions can be modeled.

self-replicating–able to reproduce independently.

stereolithography–a process for creating three-dimensional objects in which a laser beam builds a structure layer by layer.

technology–a capability given by the practical application of knowledge.

titanium–a metallic element that is very strong and lightweight.

toner–a powder used in many printers.

transplant–to move something from one place to another.

ultraviolet–relating to a type of light that cannot be seen with the human eye.

zero gravity–having no gravitational pull.

WEBSITES

To learn more about Modern Engineering Marvels, visit **abdobooklinks.com**. These links are routinely monitored and updated to provide the most current information available.

INDEX